Bees in the Attic

poems by

MaryAnn Franta Moenck

Finishing Line Press
Georgetown, Kentucky

Bees in the Attic

ACKNOWLEDGMENTS

Some of these poems have been published previously, and some appeared in slightly
different form. My thanks to the editors who published my work in these journals:

The Comstock Review: "The Dead"
Right Hand Pointing: "A single winter-brown leaf," "Pine Sap"
The Literary Bohemian: "Listening, a Guest in the Old Log House"
In the Mist: "Apple"
Cimarron Review: "American Heritage"
Water~Stone Review: "Lilacs for the Blacksmith's Wife"
Steam Ticket: "Battle Creek in Winter"

Thank you my many teachers, and to the Loft Literary Center for abundant opportunities
to nurture my writing over the years, and especially to the Loft Mentor Series.

My heartfelt gratitude to writers who have responded to my poems individually and as
part of writing groups: Thanks to my Mentor Series cohort, especially the poets, Kelly
Hansen Maher, Molly Sutton Kiefer, and Paige Riehl. And for their sustaining and good-
natured dedication to poetry I am grateful to the Bayless Avenue Poets, Naomi Cohn,
Barbara Davis, Alice O. Duggan, Ann McKinley, Lia Rivamonte, and Carolyn Williams-
Noren, all wonderful poets and great friends. Special thanks to my multi-genre artist
friend, Suzi Hudson, for her endless encouragement and friendship.
Deepest thanks to Sharon Suzuki-Martínez, my faithful and astute writing partner.
With all my heart, thanks to Jim Moenck, my blacksmith, my partner and love of my life.

Editor: Christen Kincaid
Cover Art: John J. Miller Photography, www.johnjmillerphotography.com
Author Photo: Jim Moenck
Cover Design: Elizabeth Maines

Printed in the USA on acid-free paper.
Order online: www.finishinglinepress.com
                  also available on amazon.com

Author inquiries and mail orders:
Finishing Line Press
P. O. Box 1626
Georgetown, Kentucky 40324
U. S. A.

Table of Contents

"My friends are my estate."

Emily Dickinson

A single winter-brown leaf

sweeps itself in the back door
at your heels.
You leave it on the rug,
an obsession
you can't yet banish.

The Dead

The dead don't mind if there's dust in the house. Remember,
they've agreed to this already—*ashes to ashes*. They stop by

while you are away, and adjust their own portraits
in the family gallery on your hallway wall. Their touch

leaves a little energy on the frame, a glint, favorable light
to catch your attention. For them you buy fresh flowers

every week. Beyond that, the dead want nothing. If you
love them still, they know it, and sometimes come in dreams

where they hide keys in drawers, to trunks and lacquered boxes
that you have yet to own. The dead, who finally can afford

to be lazy, are willing to work hard now, to carry all
your other griefs until you are ready to unpack them.

Some of these are new, and some too faded to name. They'll come,
help you dust them off, and put each in its proper place.

If Your Heart Is a Wayside Half-way up a Mountain

Sometimes there's mud
from travelers' boots
crusted on the wood floor.
Sometimes you sweep it clean.
Despite the mess
news is news.

Once someone stole
your sourdough (no craftsman
to fix the latch).
Another chopped wood
enough for six winters,
then left.

Log walls need repair
before the winter comes.
You might not know until spring,
when meadow flowers
bloom among the stones,
that you've slept safe.

If the chimney gets stuffed
and smoke backs up
swing the door wide. Return
and you'll see—carved there
in sunlight, all the initials
on rough wood.

Part of the Mystery

Someone milled the lumber,
forged the hasp,
planted the onion.

So easily we forget
the giving hand.

Someone pruned the pear.
Yes, someone wrote the song,
so please attend.

Night Bird

My son's in it now, running his own scam. He tells me
about his farm house north of the Cities,
and how his son has become a tree guy
like his old man. I laugh. He always defined
his livelihood as flim-flam. Trimming dead limbs
so the rest of the tree might live. *Nothing grows
up here, you know? Anoka Sand Plain,
nothing but scrub, and burr oak. The house
isn't worth much. I never had the knack
for timing, real estate deals—marriages.*
And I cannot help myself, thinking, yes
he bought the farm, the colloquial
truth. He is dying. But he loves
this place out of town. Five cats,
he tells me, *Yeah, I'm that guy.*

Once, after a spring rain, we strolled
through the night. Each street lamp
a spotlight, a new topic, the lake
murmuring alongside. *Coltrane*,
he said, and *Spider John.* Night birds.
He wanted to learn to play like that.
A lumberjack, but slighter, in suspenders
and flannel, *Do you smell that?*
What? *The basswoods in bloom—*
Point of pride, he told me: In springtime,
he could identify any native tree
in the dark. And it wasn't bragging.
He could.

The farm reminds him, he says,
of the swamps around Cromwell,
back when he was starting out.
It's like that here, in a way. You know me—
And trees. His obituary will say:
Arborist. Planner, educator,
cutting out the sick. Which they cannot do
for him, now, the disease sprawling.
Disability. A few last gigs
on Friday nights. Blues
musician. Also: Activist, poet, fierce
friend. *Nothing grows here*, he says.
He means, *No basswood.*
No sweetness. No scam
to save him now.

Listening, a Guest in the Old Log House

Early Sunday. I sit with coffee.
The dog sighs, flops before the fire,
his bones knocking on the wood floor.
The chimney of fitted stones holds rock-
memory; lapping lake, glacial flow.

A fly buzzes at the window,
takes refuge from October rain.
Dark cedar logs, hand-slabbed
long ago, are recently re-chinked.
Long wood grain emanates

the echoes of a square dance;
the wail of twin fiddles, rhythmic shuffle,
and the joining of hands. Laughter
from the baby—
her great grandpa, too.

Above the hand-hewn beams I hear
light footsteps from the bedroom.
Around the corner in the kitchen,
bacon sizzling. Two voices,
strong as ironwood, deep as pine knot:

The men, old friends. Their words
like some ancient rune, spoken low,
something about timber,
and the years it takes to season
to build a proper home.

The Poem under the Floorboards
Philip Klocksien, 1949 - 2013

During some future demolition
there will be a pause: Paper.
A poem. Anonymous, dateless,
sandwiched between subfloor and finish boards.
They won't know the poem has been ticking
there, a bomb of sentiment, since before
the world would end—this time, according
to the Mayan Calendar, winter solstice,
year-of-our-lord, 2012. They won't know
how you laughed, saying yeah, the Mayans
just got weary chiseling time
into a stone wheel. They won't know

I wrote the poem, 1988, submitted
to a contest, and won. The judge
was my idol, a demigod, whom I met soon after,
and he recalled, *Yes, the best poem
of a pretty weak field.* A middling poem, then,

the one you chose to stow for all time.
They won't know how we used to meet
for coffee, trade our work through the mail,
letters, back in the day. How we
lost touch for twenty years, until
you looked me up. That afternoon
we clung to every word, saying verses
back and forth, some immortal,
and some our own. None of it lost
on us, together at the fire until sunset.

How many years past our reunion
will the poem wait there for the light
of destruction? When they find it they will read:
Watching the Carpenter ... on good days,
he does what he said he'd do ... tearing up
subflooring to start over ... They'll see
his love of craft, and his strength.
They won't see you. Your hair fallen out,
and you still a young man. Not
your trembling hand, the spilled soup.
How you garnered your deadly
humor. The poem, hidden,
Just messing, you said, with a future
we surely wouldn't share—
How you wielded the small power
still left in you—your wit,
slow-burning.

A Dying Man Wants Poems

Is what I learned from a a dying man
who wanted poems. Beauty to match
his beauty—Acceptance. All the long
afternoon verses bounded, filled the room.
That's what I learned and thought I knew.

But *this* dying man wants something else,
or less, or different. He rages
against the respirator, the feeding tube. Look—
his swollen finger raised weakly to point
to what? A message to send,
some token to leave?

That old song, his favorite? No. To speak
and be heard—A dying man might want
justice, a cigarette, the final say.
Sedation. More of it, or less.
A memorable photo, but not that one—
It's too happy.

He raises the finger again,
and points to the can, the soda
his wife is sipping, or anything, really,
to ease the thirst, his throat raw.
He points again
to what he cannot have.

Eight days. A pyramid of empties
blocking sun from the window.
Rage, rage—
No beauty here, this poem
too late; not at all
what he wanted.

Inkwell

A squat, stoppered bottle
rests heavy on the desk.
It could hold perfume, or the genie
who already knows your wishes—
It keeps the ink, dark as a lake in a cave.

This is where they swim, the night-blind words
that nibble at the dipped nib
where it disturbs the surface, stirs
and takes what comes. You lift them, line by line
squiggling into the light.

Ice Out, Fishing in April

Silence, too, has melted.
Blackbirds cackle, and a muskrat
trembles the cattails.
Under the sky, icy privacy
has let go. You feel your skin
loosen, smell the sun on it.
With the rocking of the boat
your legs have forgotten land,
that pent up, solid place.
Geese cross over, wings whistling,
and the lake, unlocked,
riffles their reflection.
A bass makes its move,
tattled by the water's rings.

Near the sun-warm shore
the crappies have gathered
at the edge of new weeds
feeding, kissing oxygen
from the surface.
They move, eat, move. Again
the bobber dances down.
You lift another,
one of a thousand
wild and wakened lives,
up from the shallows.

Apple

Freckled red Buddha
ponders
the blossom's end,
transformed from flower
to roundness, petals
still present
as fragrance.

American Heritage

Loose curls of apple peel lie piled on the wooden board.
In half, stem to blossom end, then quarters. Quick, efficient.
With a neat turn of the knife dark seeds spill from the core.
From the quarters I slice thin longitudes. That's how
I learned geometry, I suppose, and astronomy,
at the kitchen lamp that shone on this side,
then that, of a tilted, orbiting apple.

Now, the guest of a friend, I am in another country.
Between us in her kitchen the common
geometry of a pie, and rising on the fragrance
of cinnamon, stories our grandmothers told,
tunes that both our mothers hummed.
We talk of dough proofed above a woodstove,
in simpler times how they baked *by feel*,
ingredients measured by heft in the hand.

Beside me my friend rotates the whole
apple, a globe in her hand.
She whittles little random wedges
that drop to the bowl. I watch,
proud of my own dissection of fruit—
my way faster, my friend's more relaxed,
safer perhaps; the strokes short,
the blade controlled.

Lilacs for the Blacksmith's Wife

Crooked stems drooped from the jar
where he placed them last evening,
pale blossoms limp. Of course he was tired,
having worked late at his day job.
Still, he took time to pick them
by the parking lot before he left.
He put them in water for her
while she sliced the roast.

Every spring he brings home lilacs.
This morning she dumps them all
in the sink, gathers up the blue vase,
a hammer, a cutting board,
a knife from the drawer and the steel
to sharpen it. With alternate strokes
down the long metal taper, the blade sings
an even, snick-snick rhythm.

He told her once he relishes the thought
of a woman who knows how to hone an edge.
Still, she has to bear down hard
to cut through each woody stem. Soft blows
of the hammer crush each cut end,
the pulp fraying open to thirst.

Corn Crib Shadows on the Side of a Red Barn

We stand side by side.
We have weathered
abundance and want.

Now day grows late,
fills us with light, and measures
the shadows we cast—

This is the work we were made to do:
Hold what comes.
Let it go, unspoiled.

Unseasonable Spring Heat

The birdbath has evaporated.

Irises slant with the wind, purple
blossoms darkened, withered
to ragged crepe; their long leaves
fold over gray rock
like the fingers of an old
woman who grips
the arm of her chair
where she sits, dozing.

Nearby, a fawn rests deep in shade,
born with the instinct
to press her body
against the earth
and wait.

Bees in the Attic

A load of honey, hidden.
At dusk, a soft buzzing settles,
frost on the roof.
An old woman mulls her sorrows
in her half-empty bed. Beneath
such weight, how can she rest?
Owls, a pair, calling
outside her window.

A wax candle gutters out,
smoke at the wick. Not forgetting.
Moonlight falls on a gash
in the snow, scatter of small fur.
We want long love, a circle never broken,
to live without loss. We gather,
gray as ash, warmed by a jostle of embers,
startled at our slow learning.

If the lure to a new home fails
the attic must be opened. Smoke,
and the bees re-gather, swarm
and cyclone into a clean, white box.
Still, here is the honey-comb, home
within a home, empty now.
She hears it, a buzz like a cell
in a burning log, sizzling.

Slowly, the dark dissipates,
call of the owls, the burnt-out winter—
Workmen repair her roof. Her window
opens to a warm breeze, the scent
of black earth, fields newly planted.
She bakes honeyed cornbread
for the workers. Cuts it carefully
into perfect squares.

Even a Hummingbird

after quick sips
from the impatiens'
exquisite pink

after scrapping
and chasing
at the feeder

as summer fades

must stop—

and perch
in the cherry leaves
a leaf, herself

green body
at rest.

Requiem

He loved his smokes and his salt.
His children were beans in a jar;
his daughters successful in marriage,
and his sons as kings in the koi pond.
For him there were many gods,
only one goddess.
His ears were planets. His horse
was shod and tacked with gold.

He carried a song bird, always, in his pocket.
From the corner of his eye he'd watch.
He spied the red fox
crossing over the snow
while all the skiers missed it, intent
on their poles and good form.

The journey
closed its gates,
the way a book closes
and you cannot find the page.
Such is the day we bury him:
The river threads through the village.
We gather, all of us, along the streets.

We are silent, but the houses clamor:
Shutters banging, tins in the attics
blowing off their lids.
The procession passes
and the world goes on
though we beg for it
to pause and notice.

Pine Sap

Come sit with me
beneath the trees.
They breathe,
and pump great gulps
of water up to their limbs,
engines so silent and powerful
they must weep.

Battle Creek in Winter
St Paul, Minnesota

Battle Creek flows down into Pig's Eye Lake.
Hard words for a pretty place.
The park is closed. I slip past the gate.
The frozen creek hunkers beneath limestone,
cliff-shaded from sun, stone-muffled
from the clanging rail yard
and hum of Highway 61.
I walk the park, a quiet hall apart.

I've come looking for ways to befriend
my old nemesis, two-faced god of the turning year.
He shows a cold shoulder, looking forward,
looking back, never casts an eye on here, and now—
Now January sends me aching, hinges frozen.
I drink silence, wait for something to break.

Moving waters beneath ice have a pulse, but weak.
I follow upstream. Steeper, it surfaces—
from the confusion of rapids, music.
The song struggles, lilts, and surrenders
over rocks. An eddy spins
the tentative question: Shall we continue?
Coursing bubbles slide behind a window
then dive, disappear again beneath white.

A hawk hovers high above the cliff, sun-struck.
I lift on an updraft, a prayer not my own.
Who is this, now, who prays
remembering my name?

The hushed creek gives over to greater waters,
down through the culvert under the highway,
makes for Pig's Eye and the widening Mississippi.
Down through locks and dams, takes on confluents
and Missouri mud, flows murky and rich
all the way to the silted Gulf.
Yes, we shall continue.
It is always summer somewhere.

Christmas at the Farm, and Missing You

Snow settles on the bluffs.
Snow settles on everything.
On pallets stacked
in the rail yard. On roofs, and spruce.
The Mississippi blue with ice.
A patch of open water. An eagle.
I have driven the river road,
retracing the way home until
it is part of me. The way the towns all
face the water, both sides. The way
I keep Christmas.

Fingers numb on strings still find
the chords. The way your words, always—
The way floorboards remember paint.
When woodsmoke perfumes a room
with the essence of birch.
How we used to say,
yes, next year we should ...

The farm is on high ground. I walk
toward evening, gold lingering
on tussocks, corn stubble, scalloped drifts.
Even bits of gravel cast long shadows.
I remember leaning in, fervent
for warmth. The way you
kept me. The way water seeps
through limestone. Indelible.
The way we would not say
goodbye. A kiss. See you soon.
You kept me all those years. Now

I step deep into trackless drifts.
The way I keep Christmas.
And we keep one another.
Time passes, the river,
frozen, coursing still—

MaryAnn Franta Moenck grew up east of Saint Paul, Minnesota. Gravel roads, camping with family, and gardening featured large in her childhood. Mid-way through a career in dental hygiene, she came late to poetry. She earned her BA in Creative Writing from the University of Minnesota.

Her poems have been published online, and in print journals that include *Free Verse* (now *Verse Wisconsin*), *Dogwood, Snowy Egret, Cimarron Review, Natural Bridge, Water~Stone Review,* and *Nimrod.* MaryAnn was awarded participation in the Loft Literary Center's Mentor Series for 2012-2013. She has, for several years running, been a judge for the *WriteNow!* high school writing contest, sponsored by White Bear Center for the Arts.

MaryAnn enjoys weaving, gardening, and keeping chickens. She lives with her husband on a hobby farm in rural western Wisconsin, near the St. Croix River valley.

www.ingramcontent.com/pod-product-compliance
Lightning Source LLC
LaVergne TN
LVHW091235080426
835509LV00009B/1296